A *Poet's* Diary 1

Earnest Navar Williams

To order additional copies of this book, contact:
Xlibris
1-888-795-4274
www.Xlibris.com
Orders@Xlibris.com

Acknowledgment Page:

I will like to thank God, for his support,
Without his support, this book would not be possible.

Dedication:

I like to dedicate, "A Poet's Diary 1," to the people who have inspired me directly and indirectly to be the best I could be before my community and God.

I feel honored to have crossed their paths:

Great Grandmothers; Julia Hilton, Marry Lee Turner,

And Ida Knott McClure.

Great Grandfathers; Mose W. Wyatt, Ariva Hilton and Dan Williams.

Grandmothers, Christine Wyatt and Alma Oliver.

Grand Fathers: Robert Lee Wyatt and Johnnie Walker.

Mother: Edreana Morris.

Father: Donald Williams.

Step father: Paul Morris.

My children: Earnest Novar Williams, Shakyla Novia Williams,

And Shaniya Perez.

Grandchildren: Caleb Williams, Joel Williams, and baby Perez.

Sisters: Lakreta Morris and Kristine Bostic.

Extended Brothers: Martell Love and Donald Baltic.

Nephews: Donald Ac Bostic, Corvintea Miller, Martel Love, Marc Love and Nehemiah Love.

Great Aunt: Elizabeth Travis.

Aunties: Pastor Robin Wallace, Mary Wyatt and Juila Wyatt.

Extended Aunties: Patricia Wyatt, Latanya Pitman.

Uncles: Keven Wyatt, Keith Wyatt and Michel Wyatt.

Extended Uncle: Pastor Marvin Wallace.

Extended Family: Panthia Smith, Drena Johnson, Birtha Beckley, Darlene Richards and Eugene Taylor.

Friends: Robert Bryant, Dwight Owens and Lamar Tarrant.

In addition, a host of cousins and friends too numerous to mention by name.

Organizations: Accounting Aide Society and Veteran's Educational Opportunity Program (V.E.O.P).

People Wonder Why My Eyes Red:

My eyes are red because of my dad; he is not dead.

His trait passes down the family tree:

Buried deep inside as an image to repeat,

Now, wonder no more! Wonder no more!

The trait in my eyes my father's pain, I hide.

No lying; No spoken words; and please no prying;

My red eyes do the crying,

My experiences feed what they tell.

A gaze here and there shows the feelings of hell.

A tormented body made the eyes sore.

Atlas, wonder no more, look at this picture of war:

Vessels of my eyes burst under pressure.

The pain of strain the white parts of my eyes change.

The baby grew; I no longer smile at you.

As the sunrise, the red rise in my eyes too.

I have the pain to share but care not to share it all.

I hold back pain with alcohol.

So, wonder no more!

It does not Stop Me from Being Happy:

In my mind is a maze of confusion, twisted illusions with screws missing. It does not stop me from being happy. Who am I? From where did I come? Whom can I identify with, without feeling the pain of the whip? What can I say to the masters without the whip faster? For the masters have titles: The President; The Judge; The Legislator, all police with a chain on me. For their titles, mean something to me. The effect still, I want to be free. For my mind caught between the past and the future. My eyes are looking for a solution to escape this plantation: Slavery, emancipation from the source of my confusion, the twisted illusions of freedom with the Constitution. We still have prisons and poverty like a dynasty. Is this the mark of the occupation strategy? For the strategy is with two faces. One face for someone else and one face for me- that is what I see! Even in the word, freedom is with two meanings. Both are still scheming. One meaning for someone else and one meaning for me--- I want to be free! Freedom as a verb is an illusion in motion. Therefore, here is the option. The first who make the rule win. Some-other chose the color of the tags, and we wanted the bag with the red tag. Yell we fell! Hocus pocus we lost focus! We picked the bag with the blue label, so we do not lose. Some-other made the rule; do not pick the bag with the red tag because pain will come to our head; for picking the bag with the red tag, so we pick the blue label instead. That does not stop us from paying attention when some-other chose the bag with the red tag and no pain came to their head, for picking the bag with the red tag instead. Now we have screws missing. It is not about me; it is about uplifting us and setting our sick minds free. See I am tired of hearing about the rocks and complaining about the cops adjusting with the malice intentions, to put the free mind in prison. See I am sick of hearing about the state of the union, and who to pass the onion to by organizing the black affairs. Who cares, under the United States Charter is still harder for me, but that do not stop me from being happy. My God wears the real robe. His arms spread across the expanse of the globe; as we were sold as the roll for being the property. Thank God for the all mighty. From Africa to America, the Creator was my savior. Tomorrow I do not know what the hip-hop may sing. Perhaps let freedom ring! Tomorrow, I do not know what the laws may bring. Maybe will freedom ring! What I do know, now, in my mind is a maze of confusion with twisted illusions and screws missing, but it does not stop me from being happy!

Times My Enemy:

Back then, just before the age of ten.

Time was my friend.

Days would pass without notice again,

Again, until the death of a friend name Big Ben.

I recall that changed moment,

A day of torment,

Time suddenly became worth something.

I would watch the clock,

Time would come with a tick and a tock.

Each second, valuable than the second it proceeded.

I concluded!

I live with gray hair, face wrinkles and stomach sagging.

I know death closer to coming.

I gravitate to simplicity.

It balances the effects of gravity on my body.

Each New Year marks the passage of time,

The proof, for me, times my enemy.

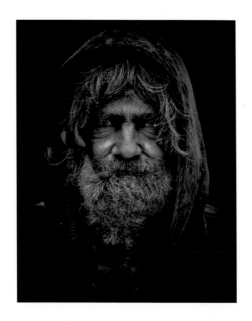

The Vagabond Was Smoking:

The bus was hot when the vagabond paid his fare.

His clothes were shabby and torn from wear.

The image of a ragged old man dressed to ruin,

He was cloth with the smell of old dry urine.

The compound of hydrogen and nitrogen turned to gas,

We could smell it as the vagabond pass.

The passengers tightly seated,

Nose clenched from the fumes heated:

Molecule ignited phlegm on their throat,

As the stink out, stinky stench emitted from his coat.

Oxygen became more valuable than gold,

They sought window control.

Shortness of breath proceeded as they retreated.

To change their disaster,

They screamed for the bus to move faster.

For the focus of their choking,

Was a vagabond smoking!

The Chosen Ones:

The constellation of Virgo did not mark the chosen one's birth.

In the heavens, Venus rising was not a sign of the chosen one's worth.

At birth, there were no gifts of frankincense, myrrh, and gold.

The chosen ones were born poor, bold and cold.

They were not born in a manger.

Some did not escape danger.

The chosen ones lived in a time of advancing technology.

Chariots of men are with a particular strategy.

Fighter Jets with men behind the trigger.

Depleted uranium shells turn humans into a crispy critter.

The planes were like horses that fly like vultures swooping to devour man.

At the same time, they were being prepared to take a stand.

The stench of death filled the air.

Some chosen one's escape death by a hair.

It was a time of a war and a riot.

Garbage scraps made up their diet,

However, they were not dismayed:

It was faith in Jesus Christ they are saved.

For it was foretold long ago, some would see this day come and go.

Jesus had lived, loved, taught and died.

He prepared a place for us in the sky.

After all Jesus have done, we were named the chosen ones.

I decided to dance:

I should have run when I had a chance.

However, I decided to dance.

She said I am her man repeatedly.

To some other, she said I am her friend,

To that end, the introduction has me hanging on
every word.

What are the true feelings behind the words I
heard?

So, who is the target?

Should I let this dance get started?

She or I who will it be.

What is the price when feelings turn to ice?

I think about tomorrow,

What should I do today?

Will she blow me away?

Nevertheless, I like her style, too soon to turn
away now!

Her sex is wild, and her smile says, "We can dance
a while."

Now I have distortions, from the fear of the ball
dropping.

Who will be sleeping?

Do I want to rest?

Oh no, I see a repeat!

I want to dance too!

The game bird I can see through,

Like a scene from a love movie, Deja Vu.

She would prove more than an ideal date:

She dresses when she should be naked.

She is naked when she should be dress,

Is that the test?

I have too many contradictions,

It feels like a love crucifixion.

I should have run when I had a chance.

But, I decided to dance!

Dream:

When my soul has surged,

It is a subconscious urge.

And during the night,

Memories form images of delight.

My mind had started the camera rolling,

Death and reality meant something.

For my cousin been dead for years,

Yet, he is alive between my ears.

I see the joy from his smile.

The visions lift me up and not down.

I feel the memories from the times that past.

I feel the love that lasts.

And during that twilight hour,

During the dreaming, I laugh at his humor:

He may not be real, as he seems.

But he is real when inside my dream!

Crack Pot!

Crack Pot is running in and out of the spot,

None stops around the clock,

Changing places changing faces,

With less time to tie his shoe laces,

Banging my ears with the sound of a screeching
doorsill, I hear.

Somebody put that Crack Pot out of his misery,

Mindset treachery!

Puff! Puff! Puff!

Crack Pot want more and more of that stuff.

He moves in and out the streets, interrupting my
sleep.

Time to stop the chain smoking.

Put an end to his tokens.

The Crack Pot was raising the roof with crack
fumes as proof.

Another Angel fell dead,

Smoking crack,

None stops, around the clock.

Halogen, pathogen, and pathologist,

Get that Angel a psychologist.

Spirited twisted mind boggles,

Angel soul tee-tar-totter,

As it descends into a speed demon,

Meanwhile, on earth, a Crack Pot is beaming.

Now I know the meaning of the phrase,

"Beam me up, Scotty!"

Another Crack Pot,

Smoking none stop, around the clock.

Crack Pot!

When I Think of Love:

When I think of love, I reflect on the heart:

As a connection between two, three and four, a swinging door.

I think of him, her, her and him, I think of them!

With love pumping through their hearts, like a flowing river full of love;

The dominant force on earth, dynamic, forever changing, rearranging, taking, destroying and hurting;

While creating, growing, nurturing, uplifting, giving, helping and loving,

I think of the heart; the principle transporter for love to start,

Love carried by the river of blood; river flowing, meandering, dissolving fears- even tears of joy, kindness, happiness, and a little madness.

Love penetrates, percolating the thin skin as sin;

Heating up and resurface as a hot spring in a summer dream; flooding with love, flowing over the surface for all eyes to see; falling from the pull of gravity,

Down the hill into a depression from all directions;

Only to confirm the presence and loss of love:

That love, I am thinking of, now divided by small rivulets;

Becoming larger as the heart moves on to another him and her; her and him,

Carrying sentiments of love memories as raging torrents that cut boulders from entire love mountains,

Leaving behind patterns of braided channels and trellis;

A heart held hostage.

Lost love new love as a river of love flows,

In the center lays the heart.

In control out of control, and covered by another lover.

That love I think of, when I think of love!

Revelation:

Revelation is like the black smoke of an inferno.

Plumes of smoke billowed out a prediction of zero.

Ambiguity rise like smoke in the codes of Revelation.

A locust come out the black smoke with its interpretation.

The interpretations are with the legion of men.

The false prophets and deceitful workers called charlatans.

Satan's disguises themselves as the angels of light.

Pillaging and ravaging the land under cover of night.

Many men fell from their dangerous and mischievous nature.

They are a troublesome **creature.**

Aristotle speaks of them as terrestrial scorpions.

Men with spirits like those who tormented Indians.

Revelation makes the terrestrial scorpions armed and dangerous.

Bible words rearranged so scorpion's announcement seem victorious.

Revelation is money made.

Revelation is commerce saved.

It smells like cinnamon and frankincense.

The interpretation of the words in Revelation is immense.

Revelation is the code language meaning danger.

Revelation word is like sounds of horns, warning, and great anger.

Revelation is like the black smoke of an inferno.

Plumes of prophesies billowed out a prediction of zero.

Revelation message is the self-destruction of men.

The cause of their implosion is the charlatan:

They are people who control others with false information.

That is the revelation!

Plant Lover Dreaming:

I close my eyes to dream.

Then, in the far away land, a baby seen.

Among the Lilac, Lily and Larkspur stand,

A white fence of petals encircles her land.

Here and there, the flowers grow fair.

Lucerne seen growing everywhere.

The flower lover of the land is honest.

She loves the land called Earnest.

Upward the stalks of Lucerne grow.

The wind blew the gold-eyed flowers bow.

In the middle of the flower, a baby wings dancing.

Then, my eyes opened to see nothing.

A plant lover was dreaming.

I am better than nothing:

I am the opposite of wrong, but I am not the best.

I am closer to the middle I quest.

I am a hero to some, to some others no identity, isolated and satanic.

I ran like a rabbit.

On the surface, I am a man with a tan,

Educated like a White man.

Disciplined like a Black man.

Slave traded, agency coordinated, felony convicted, and I do not like the disrespect.

I am the opposite of worst and less than everything, but I'm better than nothing.

A closer look, I am a war veteran that cooks.

I see images of babies do not look.

Babies' microwaved to a crispy.

The image regularly hunts me.

I see black spots on the wall:

Please do not let that be the missing body part I saw.

I struggle to keep the wall clean, and the slave trade secret.

I hope I can live this life decent.

I am the opposite of worst and less than everything, but I'm better than nothing.

Beneath the surface, I am heated.

I view myself mistreated.

While my blood is boiling, sentiments of anger are toiling.

My body feels turbulent in a cage, as my emotions expand to rage.

My eyes see the color red; as I envision those, I hate dead.

Warning, I'm about to explode,

I do not want to go down that road.

I tried to maintain control, only to lose control,

So now, I am depressed.

I suffer from Post-Traumatic Stress.

When I became homeless, I passed every drug test, but became a prescription drug addict; without it, I panic.

I am the opposite of worst and less than everything, but I'm better than nothing.

My weakness became a strength.

I am closer to God.

I am strong.

I know right from wrong.

I am the opposite of worst and less than everything, but I'm better than nothing.

Facing Slavery:

Facing slavery this coming night. O' what a fight!

The face of sweat.

Eyes of redness, watering cannot sooth it.

Tears roll from threats.

The anger I cannot hold it.

Adding more weight to a heavy collar,

Dry lumps are in my throat.

I need some water.

I am multitasking like a machine.

Still feeling like a dope on a rope.

Cannot smoke, yes, it is not a dream.

Labor for long hours and still wretched.

Money disappears like magic.

Hands blanched running at full stretch.

Captivity does not seem fair.

Nor is that slaveholder sitting in his chair,

Half man; half beast:

West meets east.

Money deafens any sounds I hear.

Even I can hear a fist full of dollars.

When applying more power,

"Wow," my loud cry becomes bleak.

Running around in circles;

Then deaf ears use more heat,

By pushing my over-worked muscles.

Got me considering another hustle.

I face slavery, this night,

I will fight thee, O' What a fight.

Pieces of God:

Before me, I see parts of God,

Right here and right now;

Not so far,

A part of God is where you are.

A piece of God is where I am.

His spirit is everywhere,

Transcending among his creation,

He is serving us with passion.

I feel real and alive,

Right here and right now;

It feels like a spring day,

My heart feels gay.

I stand among God's pieces:

Among his heavens and his earth,

Among his birds and his bees,

I stand among his trees.

When I look to tomorrow,

The earth will become new.

The order will remain with his rod.

For I know, we are all pieces of God.

On Whose Time?

On whose time shell, I climb the highest mountain,

Or arrange a garden urn,

Or drink from a spring fountain.

On whose time will I embrace the uniqueness of a fern?

Or braid your hair into a surprise,

Or turn my thoughts away from you,

On whose time shell, I open my mind's eyes,

Or set my sight on what to do;

To keep you from leaving.

On whose time shell I help others dreams come true.

Moreover, keep myself always grieving,

By holding my thoughts solely on you.

On whose time, should I have left?

One day my life will end,

I should prefer life to death.

On whose time, should I find and understand?

My spirit will depart this body torn and bruised,

Time will pass me by with each season and the weather.

While my mind betrays the body, it has used,

Imagination reveals me on many days and hours.

Therefore, it makes me wonder and see,

On whose time, you, my father's or me!

The Color of Happy:

I, too, am happy with the colors of red, white, and blue.

I am the color Red; the red stripe on the American flag.

I am the color that increases the heart rate,

I laugh with the energy, action, and passion of fireworks.

I, too, am happy with the colors of red, white, and blue.

I am the color White, the white star on the American flag.

I am the positive and adverse of all the colors.

No one dare say." Come around the back."

I, too, am happy with the colors of red, white, and blue.

I am the color Blue, the blue square on the American flag.

I am the wisdom that comes from my higher intelligence.

I am the bright blue cloudless sky.

Together red, white, and blue are the color of happy.

Tear Drops:

Sadness and sorrow produce the damage.

Tear drops falling all around here.

Saline and salty, it is falling like rain,

Even time has not made a change.

Our experiences made the teardrops heavy:

Consequences become deadly.

The clock keeps ticking it does not stop.

A reflection remains where the teardrops.

Teardrops wash away the stress.

An image of fate unfolds before us,

A weeping face the tear drops press,

Humiliation and pain are the feelings, yes!

For heavy is the weight tears drops bear,

It comes to those who care.

Oh, when tear drops fall, it pops!

Pop is the fate, of the teardrops!

I Walk with God:

I Walk with God, through the sea of the city,

My walk with God; is neither ugly nor pretty.

Willy-dilly can I see?

I must, for God to walk with me.

In faith, I surrender myself to his word,

He is Lord of Lords, have you heard?

Into his arms, I stay protected.

He orders my steps, so I feel not neglected.

In the midst of death, near and around,

A dying soul lay on the ground.

In his hand, an empty bottle of gin.

In my hand, faith cleanses my skin.

I walk with God, when times tight.

I walk with God when times right.

In the sea of the city, or abroad;

I walk with God!

Red Eyes Tell My Struggle:

If the eyes are lamps of the body,

Why my eyes so cloudy?

What set my eyes ablaze?

Is it that feeling of rage?

Alternatively, it is a fury spirit in a cage.

Pollution of the soul set my eyes ablaze.

Fire and brimstone were not a cure.

The war is keeping the body and thoughts pure.

My insides tell as the eyes show the picture of hell.

The eyes of fire, cannot hide the desire to be free,

And escape this person body, with a name like me.

I struggle with the consequences of my thinking,

My addiction for freedom has me suffering.

As a kid, I felt this addiction as a burning fire, but I was not a crier,

My gums drew blood from the gnashing of my teeth, as the pain repeat-

Turning the eyes into the flames of an inferno,

I carry fire, burning out of control, with eyes that glow:

I wish to contain the smell,

Because hell keeps the flesh burning,

Determination keeps the muscle moving, it moves, and it moves,

Its smells like old cigarettes and beer, year after year,

It numbs my suffering body and fuels the flames in my eyes.

One day this spirit will rise, and escape this burning cage of mine-

For red eyes, tell my struggle,

Bloodshot eyes show my juggle. I manipulate fire while consuming

More desires. I counter the fire in my body with a case of beer.

I drown my fire while drowning my cheer, until the passing of my body.

Then, my eyes will no longer be cloudy. The feelings will lose its rage.

When the spirit leave its cage, when the red eyes close.

The red eyes tell my struggle!

My Love Is Like the Climate of a Tropical Island, And my words are like its weather:

My love is hot, drawing the sunshine when you are near, day after day,

The warm words fall like rain as you move away.

For my love feels and looks like a tropical forest.

It is warm; it penetrates deep into the marrow of the bone.

The spongy cells have an erotic undertone.

A long-colored banana hangs in the tree.

While a beautiful flower waves its colors in the breeze,

The return of the sunshine and rain, makes nature sang.

Nature sing and it sang because my love is like the climate of a tropical island,

And my loving words fall like rain.

Puzzle:

This puzzle is a mystery I want to solve.

It could be a person, place or thing.

This thing is what have me working.

When this poem was a puzzle to me,

Problem solving came with mix feelings.

Sometimes I felt good and sometimes bad.

Sometimes I felt the best I ever had.

When this poem tested my ingenuity,

The rhythm became a puzzle to me.

What words will I find that fit?

I was amazed when I found it.

It is never a waste when a piece falls in place.

I look forward to the next puzzle.

When the pieces are together nice and neat,

If it dazzles, the puzzle becomes complete!

Jesus Paid the Price:

Jesus crucified for my redemption.

On a cross, he hung, mounted spikes in wrist and feet,

It makes me tear; images from pictures of deceit:

A crime less man died for my salvation.

The sour wine reminds me of the taste of death.

It tastes sour as vinegar.

I crave for the taste of sugar.

The craving lingers in my mouth, with each breath.

I inhale Jesus and exhale self.

His words taste sweet as honey.

They bring pleasure greater than money.

What I have left, higher than my-self.

I found redemption in Jesus.

He was the season for my reason to have hope,

As I move up and down life slope,

I have Jesus.

I can find paradise. Jesus paid the price.

God's Recipe for Love:

What recipe for love helps couples stay together for life?

Why some couples love for each other is premier?

While others live filled with hatred and strife,

And are breaking up within a year.

The answer to those questions came from the recipe above,

Some had honored God, as a husband and wife.

Like the couple who stayed together for life.

It was they, who followed Gods recipe of love.

They were practicing unconditional love,

Like their father above.

Each day, they found that perfect passion.

Passion was the foundation for a new sensation.

The feelings became the building blocks for kindness and grace.

In that grace, both found tender love and blessing above.

They had room for forgiveness when cruelty showed its face.

They escape disgrace and that bad taste.

Just like Jesus forgave those who hurt him;

The couple had looked away from the instructions of them,

They forgave each other; for them, only their love mattered.

Love is the greatest commandment of our Heavenly Father,

Anything else had led us to confusion, and strife.

At the end of the day, we were absent a husband or wife.

We had mixed ingredients such as cheating, abusing, and deceiving.

We gave the purpose of our love a smaller meaning.

The results were sexually transmitted diseases between the two.

We played peek-a-boo with love taboo while going cuckoo.

We fell to our knees unyielding; when we screamed, "God save us please."

For in our despair, forgiveness was not there.

Our prayer went unanswered, as our hearts became hardened.

We could not see, feel, hear or understand, and yet remember,

That beautiful day in December, when we first met,

Now we feel regret; counting wasted time spent.

Could we ever repent, and look to the heavens above?

Can we find God's recipe for love?

Authentic Love:

Authentic love is genuine affection without any misrepresentation.

It is courage and acceptance without reservation.

It's worthy of trust, reliance, and belief,

It is protection against grief.

It is precious to me, easy for me to see,

And should be to you too,

I hold dear an authentic love I have for you,

It is an anchor for my soul,

And away to become whole,

I trust every expression of love that proceeds from your lips,

It chips into a special feeling that tingles in my fingertips.

I rely on your authentic caress, touch, and kiss.

I am in bliss!

Our authentic love is flawlessly genuine to me.

We want to be equally happy.

The law of attraction brought us a special love.

A metaphor like a dove;

A spirit of love from high above;

It is an expression of our love filled with trust.

This love is like Earnest.

We genuinely want the best for each other.

That is our pleasure!

Come to me with that Love like God above,

Together we can claim our authentic love.

God Loves to Love:

God loves humanity because God is love.

Like renewing oxygen, it rises from the heavens above.

We inhale his love; we exhale his pleasures.

We enjoy His joys, and accomplishments beyond measure.

Love is pure; we see God's helpful, loving thoughts.

He provides all our needs, all we seek, and all we ever sought.

With or without our selfish needs and deeds,

His love allows all humanity to breathe.

Who so ever that may be; he, she, you or me, me or you!

We are the benefactors of God's labor of loves and all they do:

We bask under his sun; we shower under his rain;

We eat his fruits and vegetables and make bread from his grain.

We pick his grapes and drink up his wine.

We claim what is his; we claim it is mine.

The cause of his love keeps blessing all the time:

God's unconditional love lies within himself.

The world means more than a stone upon his shelf.

His thoughts were expressions of love, the bouquets of flowers.

The creation of woman and man, to love by his power,

Bless them; from his throne above.

While here on earth, we see God loves to love!

My life story:

My life story is a canvas of an unfinished art.

To start, vertical lines of colors, painted from the heart.

The color of red; the color of white; the color of blue;

The sections of colors that mark the spiritual times I grew.

I was born to create something profound.

Lifting up and not down, this is what I have found:

The canvas covered in red, its meaning I do not dread.

For my eyes is focus ahead, protrudes from a sea of dead.

The past mark the death and of the life of me,

I am war and the love; I am of the Calvary.

The cause of this unfinished art is time.

It takes time for the renewing of the mind.

I am the past; the present, saved by the blood of Jesus.

Thus, the light turned bright; dark set light, I stand in bareness.

Like the white background in the middle of the canvas.

I am clean from wars, guns, drugs, violence and madness.

I hope my life story ends as a beautiful masterpiece.

When my mind, heart, eyes, hands and legs cease to exist,

My hands would have been clean by the blood of Jesus.

I kill no more; I fear no more; nor cry no more; I am guiltless.

I am the color red; the color white; the color blue;

I look forward to a life made new,

In my final glory, my art is my life story.

I am done!

O my love, what have we done, to lead to this moment?

By our hands, we reap no happiness together.

By our hands, we created our torment,

By our hands, the torment is the only thing that matter.

You torment me; I torment you.

I have another lover; you have another man.

That is what we decided to do.

That is how we made our stand.

We do not like this torment coming back again.

It grows until it exposes our weakness.

We want to love again.

We contemplate our oneness.

Should we go back into the sea of no forgiveness?

We want to live, and we want to forgive.

We do not want to be destructive!

Can we get past that moment?

Yes, today we have won.

We live today, not to torment,

We live today to say, "I am done!"

The New Me:

The new me cope with my mental illness considerably.

With power, I face my illness; my actions overcome it,

Life becomes the empowering divine and the lifeline.

I emerge through an infliction, healthy and not sickly,

Into the new me; I stir, with a feeling very lovely.

I draw strength from that wonderful feeling:

Like a baby drawing nourishment from its mother breast.

Comforted by Loving feelings of the Almighty.

I am not alone; power dwells inside me.

The power to be; the power see; the power of the Almighty.

I am no longer tired, hungry, lonely or angry.

In his hands, I surrender the whole of me and am free,

As I drift toward my destiny, wherever that may be,

See me coping with my mental illness.

Feel the power that dwells within me.

Behold---The New Me!

Boy to Man:

Time has run away with me; yesterday I was a kid; today I am a man.

Among many possibilities, I stand,

Not contemplating my belief, identity, or the color of my hand.

For I am a boy to man!

In my magical moment; I feel the moment; I feel the time that past:

I feel the sadness and joys that come and go too fast.

I feel the relief, for a moment in time that did not last.

For I am a boy to man!

My magical moment came with a cause,

To think, act and speak like a man.

Here I go again, giving the reason why I took my stand.

Not contemplating my belief, identity, or the color of my hand.

For I am a boy to man!

Now understanding the power to act like a man,

Showing everyone how I live; how I aspire; how I stand,

How I use the power, I hold in my hand.

The man became a boy again, acting like a man,

I feel the power I have in my hand.

For I am a boy to man!

HALL of FAME:

Oh yeah, you are the greatest,
Like I am the greatest,
For all the things, we have done,
Oh we, we are the one,
Said those who know our name,
"You should be in the hall of fame."
Yes you, yes me, their eyes on us,
They have us feeling famous,
Oh yeah, and feeling our bloom,
Like candy in mouth with no room,
We learn to savor the flavor.
We wish fame would last forever.
See that blue sky.
See how those birds fly.
That is how we feel.
Free to know that our feeling is real.
Born to learn, learn to be born,
Live a life that is torn, and then be reborn.
Oh yeah, they all amaze,
Their eyes are in a daze.
We survived our university.
Hard knocks as they can see:

We are survivals,
Who can deny us?
That is how they know are name?
Oh yeah, we should be in the hall of fame.

Police State:

Is the United States a police state?
Eyebrows rose as we contemplate our fate.
Do we have any power?
Or is it becoming smaller by the hour?
The circle of power alludes to it's our power,
But their service to us feels and taste quite sour.
Like lemon juice without sugar.
The Police State preys on us like a cougar:
It tracks us with its mass surveillance.
It plots enslavement, death or imprisonment.
Too many laws for us to say they are on our side,
Where can we hide?
For freedom, become a mere word, and a dream.
The illusion fades away with each law they bring.
We find ourselves captives lock, stock, and barrel.
In these perilous times, who will be our hero?
The lack of freedom is the pain in our throat.
Life of hard work sacrifices and still broke.
We choke from all our rights taken.

The final force was the taking of our children.
Oh yes---It is too much for us to swallow.
A lifestyle that feels terribly hollow,
There is no substance or character in fear.
Fear brings failure and poverty year after year.
We feel the hand of the police state.
In parting freedom, we contemplate our fate.
As their system of laws turns protectors into the terrorist.
They lie, steal and imprison to maintain self-interest.
That self-interest leads, back to the police state,
Socially, economically and politically it seals our fate.
The mass populations become the cattle for the few.
Thus, a disparity in equality, what can we do?
The question comes right back at you.
What can we do?
Is the United States a police state?
Eyebrows rose as we contemplate our fate!

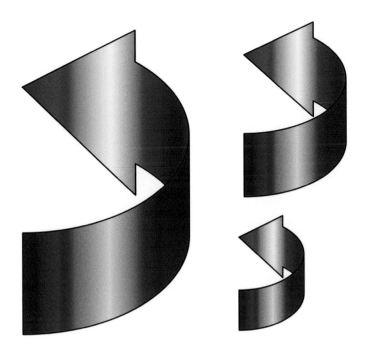

Rewind:

Rewind means to start over and become anew.

Who will erase Adam and Eve's disobedience to God?

Will it be you or me?

Oh, no we are flawed too.

Here we suffer; death we seek, until we rewind.

And undo the harm of Adam and Eve and their kind.

In a blink of an eye, we are anew.

We grow; we grew with happiness too.

No chaos; no expediency to disobedience.

For we hold the power to rewind through Jesus.

He is our past, our present, and our future,

Our peace, which brings together our pieces,

We find the path that leads back to Jesus.

Our tree connects to his root, which is how we live!

We receive the life force of Jesus when we stay in line:

The new man lives to be spiritually productive,

While the old man died, and through Jesus rewind!

God's Messengers:

God's messengers deliver messages to the world,

It echoed in the ears of a man, boy, woman, and girl.

We loved them because they practice what they preach.

Their actions were a living example of what they teach.

Their words were more valuable than a speech.

It was as good as gold as the heart God hold.

Through sight and sound, God's messengers we found.

Their message accepted in our secret place.

Beneath the wall of skin, fat, and muscle, God spirit, we face.

Among our hearts, God made his case;

Away went our selfish thoughts without a trace.

Along the path, our ego came down.

We found our hearts rooted on the solid ground.

God's messengers deliver messages to the world,

It echoed in the ears of a man, boy, woman, and girl.

We may live, or we may die, yes you will know,

And yes, will I, God is no stranger, nor is God's messengers!

Read my Mind:

Read my opinion, means to receive my thoughts,

Pure thoughts are without any cost.

The thoughts would be our gain when you discover.

Loving you is in my head,

I have a picture of you as my newlywed.

I love you to picture that in your head.

You will know your presence make me glad,

It is why I am happy and not sad.

What I want to say, my lips have not said.

Read my mind instead!

There are many reasons for my discretion.

The first reason is to clarify my intentions.

My intentions are I am sincere,

Read my mind and you will have no fear.

For I am shy; butterflies are flowing; the tongue is twisted.

Words are unsaid, daunted and halted.

If you could read my mind, what would you do?

I have a selfless love for you.

May we align, combine and intertwine---

I hope then; you could read my mind!

Tangled Web:

A tangled web is plans foiled during a scheme,

We were caught in our crossbeam,

Our self-esteem, no longer hover supreme;

Because our actions were not of our team.

If there were ever a time to beware,

What trap; what scheme;

What thought we place in our air?

It should be now!

Intent lay in who, what, when, where and how.

The web we weave for our brothers,

It is our tangled web, not any others.

What go around will come around.

What goes up will come down.

In space, in time come back regret,

Our final moments upset:

A self-inflicted stab;

While our soul is caught in our tangled web,

Too much to Handle:

A perception delivered as truthful is too much to handle.

Hurtful as a rock in my sandal;

A pin in my saddle;

Pain that is so awful, my fragile emotions cannot handle.

I retreat into safety, to be partial, and to defend my truth.

In my youth---

I am inflamed, with words that are feasible before my endnote.

I do not like people perceptions force down my throat!

As an antidote, my tongue ignites against others perception.

Words become flames and burn without discretion.

I forget about the figures,

Or the threat that someone may pull the trigger.

I hear no angels in my battle: I see my evil,

I feel my trouble that busts my bubble:

A perception delivered as truthful---

It is too much to handle!

Excuse:

Oops, another excuse again, and I know how that look.

His image is like a bird with a broken wing and easy to cook.

For the picture of the man died with every excuse.

He withered away, and the bird that remained was his truce.

To be more specific, his "will" ended before the fight,

I heard the sound of a real chicken tonight.

Ro-uh-Ro-uh-Roo, the excuses moved forward,

Sound waves bring feelings of resembling a coward.

I do not like those feelings, for him or me.

The feelings break me down as far as I can see.

That lame excuse upsets my stomach.

I want to say, "Get away before I vomit."

The cause of my illness, stem from the excuses I hear.

The sound tells me he is near.

He has an excuse for this, and he has an excuse for that.

That is how an excuse maker reacts.

I hope I can find my truce,

And ignore his same old excuse!

Kicking the boa boas:

Kicking the boa boas becomes entertainment.

The entertainment is in the story and phrases,

The way phrases are in the arrangement,

It portrays the old news; new news, during the display;

Among family and friends, kicking the boa boas makes our day.

We laugh; we joke; we drink; we smoke,

The more we laugh, the more we joke!

We feel what we say, down to the tip of our toes,

We move among family and friends kicking the boa boas.

For we know--- what boa boas we are hearing sound not true.

It is what they said, how they said it, and what they do.

They make us think--- They believe what they say is true.

They cannot help but keep their eyes on us too!

Imagine the whole world kicking the boa boas.

No cues predispose; decreased woes; happiness arose,

Our face glows; for we all are kicking the boa boas.

Picture of You:

A picture of you plays in the front of my head.

Scene by scene what you did,

What you said created this image in my head:

I can see the innocence of a child.

As your smile light, up the background, it drives me wild.

I think I am in love again.

You look happy being in love with this friend.

I think good things about that picture playing in my head.

You are the best thing I ever had.

I have no reason to be sad.

I have your picture in my head.

In this midnight hour,

One of the times, I felt your power.

A trigger---Oh! While in a cold shower.

A bar of soap become a memory I knew.

I recall that picture of you.

I remember what I had.

I remember that picture in my head.

I wish I could see you again; hold you tight,

I want to love you with all my might.

I wish I could see you from another view,

Not just from that picture of you!

Ahhh...

Ahhh... is a sound we hear, when we hit that spot.

Are we a bore? "Oh no," we are not!

Ahhh... is saying," Please don't stop."

We keep on ticking like a clock.

We love it...We love it; we are here to please;

We go with the flow as their demands we appease,

Adrenaline surged, as the peak comes in threes.

Ahhh... is the sound from a vocalese---I believe.

And the rise to crescendo;

Where this pleasure flow:

From the do-SE-do, mix with our libido,

Cause the climaxes to follow; it justifies our bravado.

Ahhh...It makes us smile,

To know we brought that gush down.

Over and over, around and around,

When we hear that sound, "Ahhh..."

Psychosis:

Psychosis is a condition of the mind;
The mind is out of place and out of time.
The body is home, but the reality is gone.
The contact with reality end at a cost.
What went wrong?
The mind plays its song!
Hallucination got me playing along,
Sounds in my head have me talking out of key.
People are wondering what is wrong with me.
I talk to others; people cannot see,
Delusions have a hold on me.
Mental chain some others can see.
While reality fades into uncertainty,
Psychosis has me feeling my doom.
Bombs are blasting in my room.
Boom! Boom! Boom!
I am dying much too soon.
While in my damaged tomb,
I sleep all day and hear bombs during the night.
My body is tired; I am in a constant fight.
How do I get pass the hallucination?

Or pass this marijuana intoxication?
For I smell dead bodies in my head,
My fingers reap with the smell of a pothead.
I hope I don't choke from all that marijuana smoke.
And I find a door out of this mind of war.
Finally, I will awake to see the light,
And my nights will feel bright.
That will be my time, my diagnosis,
Would no longer be psychosis!

Eustress:

Eustress is another word for real stress.

Positive pressure is the motivation to move forward.

It is awkward to stand still when you feel Eustress.

Our gaze followed skyward.

We feel we can touch that sky.

Positive stress has us feeling our best.

Our best is with that natural high.

Prepared are we for that test, yes!

Adrenaline flows into our blood.

Our heart beats a lot faster.

We feel the flood.

Our senses become our master.

It strips away our fears,

As we accept success,

We feel the power of Eustress!

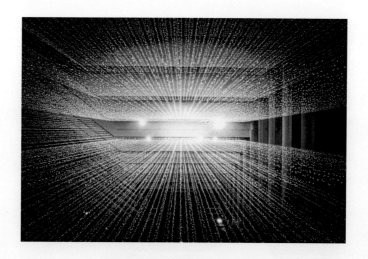

Police Violence:

Bang--- Bang--- Bang--- The sound of gunshots rang.

A defenseless person of color shot dead by police,

He falls off his feet; on the ground, he lay deceased,

We see the shooter was a police.

Police---Police---Police, your eyes are cold,

Cold as the reason your eyes were fishing.

We could feel your soul hissing.

The benevolence in your manner was missing.

Where is the humanly remorse?

No change of your abusive course.

What do we do about that police violence?

It robs us of life, liberty, and pursuit of happiness.

It creates an environment of fear and madness,

It leaves us looking down at the ground.

A shell of what is there now found.

Another black soul rose up and forced down.

Down---Down---Down---

His body lay motionless on the ground.

The protector became the hunter and the killer.

We are wondering when freedom will ring,

When God shows his hand of benevolence,

And finally, end our police violence.

Keep on walking:

Keep on walking means to keep going.

When today's struggles feel heavy on our back,

And confusion keeps us off track.

We must not look back just keep on walking.

Away, away, we like it like that.

The way we walk, not mad or sad,

Or letting those struggles get in our head.

We kept on walking instead and did not get upset.

We set ourselves for better days coming by,

Out with the struggles and in with feeling alive.

We survived all that jive!

We said bye---bye---bye.

We look forward to the happy days coming.

In our confusion, we did learn:

Chaos will change, and struggles will return.

To keep striving, we must keep on walking.

Out Cold:

Out cold is a term we use to express an impression.

The impression we receive is either bad or good;

We express those feelings in the hood.

To be understood, we must use out cold with discretion.

We learned that lesson when we use the term before.

Out cold is bad when misunderstood.

It can happen when the phrase used outside the hood.

So, to stay on the neutral side of the door;

We feel we could and should define what it means.

Who so ever is out cold, they are what they seem.

They appear to benefit only themselves to the extreme.

They draw our attention like a telephone ring:

For their personality rang in our memory.

Their action is bold when we say, "They're out cold."

We watch as their personalities unfold.

Like the people next door who killed the family of three.

We were traumatized by their savagery.

The action behind what they did; we did comprehend.

We look to a term to express that cold feeling within.

The expression was there for ears to hear and eyes to see.

Self-interest meets bold and their personality unfold.

What we see, feel and hear is out cold!

Anticipation:

Anticipation, I look forward to our first date.

My heart, mind, and soul anticipate.

I think over and over again our fate.

I celebrate; my love will not arrive too late.

I wait, and I hold on, with feelings of excitement,

In my cheer, as time draws near, my endearment;

Happy feelings flow, as I go, into that moment.

Time and space bring forth excitement.

And in between that time and space,

In my mind, I recreate, repeatedly, your face,

My passion silently assumes its place.

I visualize your kiss and the bliss of its taste.

I celebrate; my love will not arrive too late:

It is with anticipation, I wait!

AS ONE:

My love! My love! Look at what happiness has done!

We have become as one,

You and me; me and you; our hearts blend too;

Together, as one, that is when happiness show through.

I feel as one with that feeling within you.

Happiness brought together the souls of two.

We feel complete; we feel the glee;

We feel the feeling of being exclusively happy.

Love is the cause of that happy feeling.

It brings together two persons caring.

You care for me; I care for you;

That is what we, who truly are happy, do,

And in the midst of our life changes,

Love grows and rearranges.

It collaborates as it bends.

We comprehend what this love is.

It is you and me, you and I, in matrimony.

We love each other along life journey.

We harmonize our soul, body, and mind.

This is what we have with time:

My love, two hearts, became as one.

Look at what true love has done!

A Poop Relationship:

Poop is the waste from the digestive tract.

How does poop in a relationship interact?

It is the digestion of a wasted mind,

When poop in a commitment is a waste of time,

I could feel the poop between her and me.

Her face, "Wow," I can see.

The deck piled to the sky,

Do I clean it, no, not I?

I see her poop face,

The smell, I can imagine how it tastes.

The poop smells somewhat fishy.

Could it be me, or my messy?

Do you know what I mean?

Someone else has come in-between.

Now I am reminded of the cause.

Was it the poop defecated from the jaws?

There was no value in the words.

Death to that relationship is what I heard.

Dead bacteria made the commitment smell.

Oh well, let's run like hell;

Farewell to the tears and the worries,

Bury that poop in a hurry.

I offer you this tip:

Avoid a poop relationship.

Comforter:

O my Comforter, I welcome your comfort,

Like I welcome a warm blanket on a cold day.

The flame of your way comforts me, what else can I say.

As ice melt before a fire, my fear melts before you.

I can feel your touch, my comforter, O yes, I do.

I feel the power of your gentle flame.

I feel secure, for I know by whom you came.

You came from God; I know that to be.

For in my lowest moment, you comfort me.

Your words were smooth as butter,

I hear, so clear, and I felt better.

My spirit arose as I surrender to the sound.

Vibrations of joy pour from the heaven down:

My Creator, my Savior; becomes my Comforter:

My handclap in victory;

For I see, fear has no hold on me.

Seduce me:

I seduce you, oh no, that's not fun;
You seduce me, oh yeah yum, yum, yum.
I cannot resist the lust in your eyes,
Or the chocolate scented covered thighs.
I can feel the passion from your flesh.
Each touch becomes a magical moment.
Your hands fondle my body here and there,
I can feel the fondling everywhere:
Like my thighs, stomach, chest and neck;
Your touches got me wanting your sex.
I want to consume you more and more.
The whole of you has opened the door.
I see your heart burns to be with me,
It cooks to make your dream come true.
My mind sizzle for that moment,
Where passion has influenced my judgment:
Take my mind; my body; and my soul;
Today, I surrender to your control.
I do not care what people say or see,
Just seduce me!

Printed in the United States
By Bookmasters